INSIDE TRACK
TO THE TRIPLE CROWN

INSIDE TRACK
TO THE TRIPLE CROWN

*Everything You Need to Know
About the Kentucky Derby,
Preakness & Belmont Stakes*

For Fans, Fanatics & First Timers

PHOTOGRAPHY BY
Anita Scialli

TEXT BY
Anita Scialli
as told to
MaryAnn Hagerty
& Joseph Avenick

CORMORANT PRESS
PHILADELPHIA

CORMORANT PRESS, LTD.
842 South Second Street, Suite 351
Philadelphia, PA 19147
(215) 922-3009

The publisher welcomes comments and suggestions for future editions
of *Inside Track*. Please contact us at the address and phone listed above.

This book is intended as a recreational and informational guide.
It should not be considered an endorsement of any horse or person.

First Edition 1997
Published and bound in the United States of America

Library of Congress Cataloging-In-Publication Data.
Scialli, Anita as told to Hagerty, MaryAnn and Avenick, Joseph
Inside track
Anita Scialli as told to MaryAnn Hagerty and Joseph Avenick
ISBN 1-885884-25-7
Library of Congress Catalog Card Number: 97-66666

Photographs by Anita Scialli
Cover & Book Design by Doreen Naughton/Cormorant Design

With a world of love and respect,
this one's for you, Mom and Dad

ACKNOWLEDGMENTS

To the six of us who were together once upon a time not so long ago when this book took its first breath of life (Mary, MaryAnn, Doreen, Joe, me and my dog Nikki).

Special thanks to Carolyn and Dan for getting me on "the right track" and continuing to put up with myself and Nikki year after year as Triple Crown seasons come and go. Also, many thanks to the south Florida starting gate crew; and to my agent, Steve Dalton.

TABLE OF CONTENTS

HOW'D THEY GET HERE?

The Kentucky Derby, the Preakness, and the Belmont Stakes are the most famous horse races run in America and, collectively, are known as the Triple Crown. This book will give you some interesting information about the Triple Crown races in particular and horse racing in general. Throughout the book, you will see words printed in bold. These words have special meaning in the sport of thoroughbred racing and are defined in the **Horse Talk Glossary** at the end of the book. If you are an ordinary fan or a first timer, you will find that all the sections of *Inside Track* will help you understand and enjoy the races. If you're a fanatic, you already know most of these facts, or think you do, so you may choose to skip to the write-ups of the contenders (page 15).

The first of the Triple Crown races, The Kentucky Derby, takes place on the first Saturday of May in Louisville, Kentucky. The Preakness, in Baltimore, Maryland, comes two weeks later; and the Belmont Stakes is run in Elmont, New York, three weeks after the Preakness. Of the three races, the Kentucky Derby is by far the most famous; but a horse must win all three in order to capture the Triple Crown.

How do horses get to the Triple Crown races? It's a struggle. Only three-year-olds may run, and usually it takes the good part of a year to narrow the field down to the best of the pack.

Everything starts with good breeding, paying very close attention to the father and the mother. Horses are like people. They can be **sprinters** or distance runners. With some luck and good planning, they may be born to win, make lots of money, and make even faster babies.

Every horse celebrates his or her birthday on January first of each year. The breeding season is planned when the reproductive systems are in highest gear. Most foals are born between January and June, but whatever the birth date, they all become one year old on the same day: January first. So it's possible to have as much as five months difference in the true age of these horses grouped together as three-year-olds.

Party Animal

According to horse tale tradition, every race track in North America throws a birthday party for the horses on the eve of their universal birthday. Reportedly, the horses celebrate with birthday cake, streamers, hats, and chocolate-covered oats.

Horses who compete in the Triple Crown start their racing careers once they've been **broken** to accept a saddle and rider, worked out and conditioned daily, clocked for speed, **vetted out**, and checked for **soundness.** A horse's childhood can be traumatic, because he may have been sold to new owners, have new trainers, new exercise riders, or get shipped to a different part of the country.

A horse begins racing against horses of similar capability and approximately the same age. The ability to run longer distances at peak performance and speed often distinguishes champions from also-rans. Girls and guys occasionally run against each other throughout their careers; however, very few **fillies** have competed in, or won, the Kentucky Derby. Only three fillies have won the Derby: REGRET in 1915, GENUINE RISK in 1980, and WINNING COLORS in 1988. Although there is no true sexual discrimination in entrance requirements, it's usually guys competing against guys in the run for the roses on Derby day.

On the day before the Derby, many of the top three-year-old

fillies run for the lilies in the Kentucky Oaks race. For those in the know, both races are meaningful and a great honor to win, but only the winner of the Derby gets most of the recognition and a chance at the Triple Crown.

A thoroughbred's racing career begins as a two-year-old and proceeds as a type of elimination process. The winners of certain races are entered into races with higher **purses**, thus going up the ladder. When they prove themselves, eventually they enter **stakes** races. The best stakes races are graded as follows:

Grade III: Lowest of the important stakes races
Grade II: The next rung up
Grade I: The most money/prestige

As the size of the purse increases, so does the level of competition. The Kentucky Derby (often called the greatest two minutes in sports) is the most important Grade I race for three-year-olds, because if you don't win that one, you have no chance of capturing the Triple Crown.

Why is the Triple Crown so coveted? Partly because it has seldom been won. There have been only 11 Triple Crown winners in all the years of racing. Then there is the prestige to have owned, trained, ridden a Triple Crown winner. If the horse is good enough to win these three tough races, the horse may also win a great deal of money in other races. Finally, there is a fortune to be made in putting the horse out to stud; that is, to be the **sire** or **dam** of future winners.

Some owners, trainers, and jockeys work a lifetime and never earn the honor or privilege of running a horse in the Kentucky Derby. Many compete, but only an average of 12 to 14 of the best break from the starting gate of the most publicized race of the year.

Owner and trainer relationships are important in the well being and progress of the horse—which must perform at maximum potential when it counts. The horse must be in top condition. Sometimes, a horse may be hurt the day before one of the big races, develop a fever, or stumble coming out of the gate. It is heartbreaking for something to go wrong after all the hard work of getting to a Triple Crown race. For example, TIMBER COUNTRY, a top contender for the 1995 Belmont Stakes, was **scratched** because he developed a fever the night before the Saturday race. This was a huge disappointment to his **connections**. This scratch of a favorite horse also altered the betting pattern of the fans.

All the hopefuls want a chance to win the Triple Crown, but only one can: the winner of the Derby, who then wins the Preakness, and then wins the Belmont Stakes. It is a small, highly elite club. These are three grueling races which take a lot out of a horse, and only the strongest and most fit can withstand the rigors of the training necessary to stay in top condition and compete in three races within five weeks in three different states on three tracks with vastly different surfaces. The winner has to be a well-rounded, adaptable horse, because many factors impact performance. The weather can be a major influence on the race: rain or high wind, or even a sunny day, all affect a horse's performance. Breeding can also affect which conditions horses prefer. Some run better on muddy tracks; some on dry; some like the heat; some don't sweat, so they run better in cold weather. All of these factors together make a big difference in major races. For example, GO FOR GIN beat TABASCO CAT on Derby day in 1994 running in about six inches of sloppy mud because of torrential rains; but with dry weather, TABASCO CAT went on to win the Preakness and the Belmont. A fine horse named CIGAR never entered the Triple Crown because his breeding was for **turf** racing; however, when he turned four, his owners tried racing him on the dirt, and he couldn't be beat. Some horses just have heart.

The rigorous road for 1997 has been paved. Presented in this book are the proven fastest of the current three-year-old population. Herein are the best of the best. They have earned their way into the spotlight.

KEY PREP RACES

Prior to the Triple Crown series, three-year-olds will compete in other stakes races throughout the country. Purse money in each of these preps will run from $50,000 to $750,000—not exactly a small consolation prize. Most of the following prep races, which are contested in January through April, have long-respected traditions of their own. The distance of each varies from seven **furlongs** to a mile-and-an-eighth. Not one will equal the distance of any Triple Crown race.

Arkansas: Arkansas Derby, Southwest Stakes, The Rebel
California: California Derby, San Felipe Stakes, San Rafael
            Stakes, Santa Anita Derby
Florida: Hutcheson Stakes, Holy Bull Stakes, Fountain of
            Youth Stakes, Florida Derby, Flamingo Stakes
Kentucky: Jim Beam Stakes, Lexington Stakes, Blue Grass
            Stakes, Derby Trial (the final prep, one week
            before the Kentucky Derby)
Louisiana: Louisiana Derby
Maryland: Federico Tesio Stakes
New York: Gotham Stakes, Wood Memorial

In addition, England has its own "Kentucky Derby Prep" race for those horses considering the transatlantic trip. Other parts of the U.S. and Canada will also have three-year-old races that can be used as stepping stones to the Triple Crown.

1997 SCHEDULE
OF TRIPLE CROWN RACES

May 3:   Kentucky Derby, 1 1/4 miles
Churchill Downs Race Track
Louisville, Kentucky
Purse: $1 million

May 17:   Preakness Stakes, 1 3/16 miles
Pimlico Race Track
Baltimore, Maryland
Purse: $500,000

June 7:   Belmont Stakes, 1 1/2 miles
Belmont Park Race Track
Elmont, New York
Purse: $500,000

BLANKETS OF FLOWERS
FOR THE WINNER

Kentucky Derby:	Roses
Preakness Stakes:	Black-Eyed Susans
Belmont Stakes:	Carnations

PREVIOUS TRIPLE CROWN WINNERS

1919	SIR BARTON
1930	GALLANT FOX
1935	OMAHA
1937	WAR ADMIRAL
1941	WHIRLAWAY
1943	COUNT FLEET
1946	ASSAULT
1948	CITATION
1973	SECRETARIAT
1977	SEATTLE SLEW
1978	AFFIRMED

OWNERS, TRAINERS & JOCKEYS

Owners

Buying a racehorse isn't cheap. That's putting it mildly. To purchase a young, unraced thoroughbred with the breeding potential of a Triple Crown winner can cost an average of $400,000. However, there are bargains. SEATTLE SLEW, the 1977 Triple Crown winner, cost only $17,000. Some owners have farms where they breed the best stallion they can afford to the best mare they own. Jack and Catherine Price paid $150 to buy a mare, JOPPY, whom they then bred for free to the stallion, SAGGY. The SAGGY/JOPPY coupling produced CARRY BACK, who went on to win the 1961 Kentucky Derby and Preakness, as well as over $1.2 million.

To keep a horse in training can cost an owner from $2,000 to $3,000 per month. This starts the domino effect that keeps trainers, jockeys, grooms, veterinarians, and others employed, and even helps race tracks put on a show.

Success as an owner can come quickly, slowly, or not at all. Owner Fred Hooper's first horse, HOOP, JR., won the 1945 Kentucky Derby. Hooper's subsequent horses have won numerous stakes races, but not another Kentucky Derby. Hooper, who will turn 100 years of age in October, is still seeking Derby win number two.

Mrs. Frances Genter had owned thoroughbreds for over 60 years without a Kentucky Derby winner until her UNBRIDLED won the 1990 Run for the Roses. In one of the most heart-warming scenes in racing history, the 90-year-old Mrs. Genter, with failing eyesight, was standing near the finish line alongside her trainer, Carl Nafzger, while the horses raced through the homestretch at Churchill Downs. Mrs. Genter listened, with tears of joy, as Nafzger described how UNBRIDLED was moving from far back in the pack of horses to take the lead and then win the Kentucky Derby.

Trainers

Trainers come from all walks of life. They may have doctorates, or be high school dropouts. Yet they all seek the same thing—one good horse.

Thoroughbred trainers are morning people, out of necessity. Whether they train just one horse or several dozen, they must be at their stables before dawn to supervise their horses' exercise regimens. They must deal with jockeys, agents, grooms, feed salesmen and, of course, horse owners. The tension starts early and lasts until late afternoon, when one of their horses may lose a race by the bob of a nose.

Trainer Michael Trivigno

In the first half of this century, Ben and Jimmy Jones trained for Warren Wright's powerful Calumet Farm, which dominated Triple Crown racing with such champions as WHIRLAWAY and CITATION. In the past decade, trainers Darrel Wayne Lukas and Nicholas P. Zito have been the most successful. Lukas trained the filly, WINNING COLORS, who won the 1988 Kentucky Derby. He also trained the winners of six straight Triple Crown races from 1994 to 1996. Zito won the 1991 Kentucky Derby with STRIKE THE GOLD, the 1994 Kentucky Derby with GO FOR GIN, and the 1996 Preakness with LOUIS QUATORZE. But quite possibly the Triple Crown training record that will never be broken is held by Woodford Cefis Stephens. "Woody" trained the winners of the Belmont Stakes five years in a row (1982-1986).

Trainer John Ward, Jr., whose farm abuts Keeneland Race Course in Lexington, Kentucky, comes from a long family line of thoroughbred trainers. "After many years, I was lucky enough to have two starters in the Kentucky Derby [1995: JAMBALAYA JAZZ and PYRAMID PEAK]," Ward stated. "And I realize it may take me another lifetime before I have a horse good enough to run in a Triple Crown race."

Jockeys

Bill Hartack, Eddie Arcaro, Willie Shoemaker. These Hall of Fame riders were synonymous with Triple Crown racing in the recent past. Today's riding heroes include the likes of Jerry Bailey, Pat Day, and Chris McCarron.

A jockey at work

Starting at the bottom, most jockeys clean stalls, walk horses, and ride them in morning workouts. In the beginning of their careers, they are all given slow horses to ride. Then, gradually, as they showcase their skills, their services become in greater demand. Just as the field of Triple Crown horses is narrowed down, so are the jockeys.

Jockey Julie Krone is recognized as a top American rider. She is the only woman to have won a Triple Crown race—the Belmont Stakes aboard COLONIAL AFFAIR in 1993. She started her career at tracks such as Atlantic City Race Course (New Jersey) before moving on to major meets such as Saratoga and Belmont (both in New York), where she rides regularly.

In a typical year, a top jockey who rides frequently will have about a thousand or so mounts. With luck and a reputation based on skill, three of these will be in Triple Crown races. A win on any of the three will make up for all those rainy, cold and snowy race days; all of those hard surfaces felt when dumped by a horse; and all those nagging injuries.

As jockey Pat Day says, "Many spectators feel the 20 to 30 minutes between races is a long time, but for a jockey it is a very short span allowed for mental preparation. If the jockey wins the race, there are only moments to savor the success—and if a losing or poor race is run, there are only moments to get back the self-esteem and confidence and to ride a better race next time out. Football players have a week to recover, we don't. The emotional roller coaster is constantly on the move."

BETTING TIPS

Be aware of a track "bias." This is a condition that favors either a certain post position or a certain type of running style. For example, on rainy days, posts one and two usually have an advantage at Aqueduct Race Track. Probably the most pronounced bias in many years was evidenced at Gulfstream Park during the 1997 meet when horses who showed early speed had a tremendous advantage over horses with late speed. This Gulfstream Park bias should be noted by bettors. When horses with late speed are then moved to a fair racing surface at another track, their performance will improve dramatically.

Watch the odds board. Compare the "guesstimated" odds in your program with actual odds during the wagering period just prior to a race. If, for example, a horse who was thought to be a 5 to 1 shot is now only 2 to 1, this is evidence that he is highly thought of and may run much better than most pundits had predicted.

Look at the horses in the **paddock** and when they parade in front of the stands prior to the race. Male horses who are sweating are generally not good bets. Horses who hold their heads low, and who are walking without any noticeable limping, are usually good bets.

When a horse drops in class (for example, to a lower **claiming** price), it is usually a good bet only if its previous race has been run within two weeks, and it is being ridden by one of the meeting's leading riders. If a horse is running for the first time with **blinkers**, he is often an excellent bet. Horses who are running with the anti-bleeding medication Lasix (furosemide) for the first or second time are usually good bets. The daily program will note whether horses are on the medication.

How to Place a Bet

First Step: open wallet, shake hard.

Don't be intimidated when you approach a betting window to risk your hard-earned cash. Remember that most tracks accept bets for races run at other locations, so you need to specify the name of the track where your horse is running. Just tell the clerk, in this order, what you want:

Name of the racetrack at which your horse is running.
The number of the race on which you are betting.
The amount of your bet.
The type of bet. The simplest types of bets are:
   Win (the horse must come in first),
   Place (the horse may come in first or second), and
   Show (the horse may come in first, second or third).
Number of the horse on which you want to bet.
   This number is shown to the left of your horse's name on the racing program.

An example of a simple bet for the Kentucky Derby would be: Churchill Downs, Race 8, $2 to Win on Number 4. (This is not an endorsement, just an example.)

THE 1997 CONTENDERS

There are many more horses presented here than could possibly compete in the Kentucky Derby, and there are two good reasons for this. First, some horses develop later than others and may not be ready to race in the Derby but are ready some weeks later to compete in either the Preakness or the Belmont Stakes (or both). Second, some horses do better in longer distance races and therefore are pointed to the Belmont rather than the Derby. So, in order to provide a complete guide, we are listing the horses that may eventually appear in at least one of the Triple Crown races.

Running a horse in these races isn't cheap. For the Kentucky Derby, an owner has to pay $30,000 to see his horse run around the track whether he finishes first or last. For the Preakness, it's $15,000. For the Belmont Stakes, it's $10,000. Such is the price of potential fame. If you win all three races, your purse winnings will be over a million dollars, and your horse will be worth multiple millions when retired for breeding purposes.

The 1997 contenders are presented in alphabetical order. We considered grouping them in categories such as "Favorites," "Real Contenders," and "Long Shots," but it's been 18 years since a favorite won the Kentucky Derby (SPECTACULAR BID in 1979). So you can see how "useful" the groupings would have been. Therefore, the horses are presented in alphabetical order with comments on their performances in prep races along with other topics of interest.

Good luck!

ACCELERATOR

Sire   A. P. INDY
Dam   GET LUCKY
Owner   Ogden Mills Phipps
Breeder Ogden Mills Phipps
          (bred in New York)
Trainer   Claude McGaughey

ACCELERATOR won the 1996 Pilgrim Stakes at Belmont (Elmont, New York). McGaughey saddled EASY GOER to second place in the 1989 Kentucky Derby and Preakness. EASY GOER then won the 1989 Belmont Stakes.

ACCEPTABLE

Sire   CAPOTE
Dam   MS. TEAKWOOD
Owner   Kinsman Stable and
          Three Chimneys Farm
Breeder Kinsman Stud Farm
          (bred in Kentucky)
Trainer   Nicholas P. Zito

In 1996, ACCEPTABLE finished second to BOSTON HARBOR in the $1 million Breeders Cup Juvenile at Woodbine in Canada. In 1997, he finished second to ARTHUR L. in the Holy Bull Stakes at Gulfstream Park (Hallandale, Florida). ACCEPTABLE's trainer, Nicholas P. Zito, trained LOUIS QUATORZE, who won the 1996 Preakness. Kinsman Stud Farm is owned by George Steinbrenner, whose New York Yankees won the 1996 World Series.

AMERICAN CHAMP

Sire	JOLIE'S HALO
Dam	HEART OF AMERICA
Owner	Arthur I. Appleton
Breeder	Arthur I. Appleton (bred in Florida)
Trainer	Robert W. Camac

In 1997, AMERICAN CHAMP won the Best Turn and Fred Caposela Stakes at Aqueduct (Ozone Park, New York) both at the six-furlong distance. He is a grey and has been ridden by Tony Black, the all-time leading jockey in number of victories at Philadelphia Park (Bensalem, Pennsylvania).

ANET

Sire	CLEVER TRICK
Dam	ROMANTIC STORY
Owner	Double Diamond Farm
Breeder	D. W. Frazier (bred in Florida)
Trainer	Bob Baffert

ANET defeated FUNONTHERUN last year at Del Mar, California. In his first 1997 race, he lost to P.T. INDY and KING OF SWING at Santa Anita (Arcadia, California). In his next start, he was an easy winner in the Rushaway Stakes at Turfway Park (Florence, Kentucky), with IN CC'S HONOR finishing second.

ARTHUR L.

Sire	OCALA SLEW
Dam	WILLIE'S COBRA
Owner	Cobble View Stable
Breeder	Beeler Enterprises (bred in Florida)
Trainer	Luis Olivares

ARTHUR L.'s sire never raced. However, ARTHUR L. won the What A Pleasure Stakes in 1996 at Calder Race Course (Miami,

Florida) by 17 lengths. He then won the first Derby of 1997, the Tropical Park Derby (also at Calder) on January 2nd of this year. Soon after, he won Gulfstream Park's (Hallandale, Florida) Holy Bull Stakes, defeating ACCEPTABLE and CAPTAIN BODGIT. Olivares: "He hurt a leg in March when he got tangled in the web in his stall. He might be able to make the Belmont."

BLAZING SWORD

Sire	SWORD DANCE
Dam	DEMETROULA
Owner	Stonehedge Farm
Breeder	G.G. Campbell (bred in Florida)
Trainer	Kathleen O'Connell

BLAZING SWORD won two Florida Stallion Stakes races last year at Calder Race Course in Miami. The gelding finished second at Keeneland (Lexington, Kentucky) in the Breeders Futurity to last year's two-year-old champion, BOSTON HARBOR. In 1997, BLAZING SWORD finished second to PULPIT at Gulfstream Park (Hallandale, Florida) in the Fountain of Youth Stakes. Gary Boulanger and Abdiel Toribio rode BLAZING SWORD in his most impressive races.

MANUAL DELAY SWITCH

Did you know that, instead of windshield wipers, jockeys wear up to five pairs of goggles on rainy days and take them off, one by one, while they're racing. We assume the poor horses blink a lot.

CAPTAIN BODGIT

Sire	SAINT BALLADO
Dam	ANSWERING ECHO
Owner	Team Valor
Breeder	Edward Wiest (bred in Florida)
Trainer	Gary Capuano

CAPTAIN BODGIT won five races in a row in 1996, topping off the year with a victory in the Laurel Futurity. He suffered poor starts in his first two races of 1997, the Holy Bull and Fountain of Youth Stakes at Gulfstream Park (Hallandale, Florida), finishing third both times after rallying late from far off the pace. In the Florida Derby at Gulfstream Park, CAPTAIN BODGIT put in a furious late run to pull away from PULPIT and cross the finish line more than two lengths in front. CAPTAIN BODGIT was purchased by Team Valor for $500,000 after his race in the Holy Bull. HALO, the grandsire of CAPTAIN BODGIT, is a half brother to 1963 two-year-old filly champion, TOSMAH, who went on to become one of the greatest racemares in the history of the American turf. On April 12th, with Alex Solis riding, CAPTAIN BODGIT took to the water-covered Aqueduct racetrack like a cormorant splashing through the ocean—winning the Wood Memorial easily over ACCELERATOR.

CONCERTO

Sire	CHIEF'S CROWN
Dam	UNDENIABLY
Owner	Kinsman Stable
Breeder	Kinsman Stud (bred in Kentucky)
Trainer	John Tammaro III

CONCERTO earned over $214,000 in 1996, winning the Storm Cat Stakes at The Meadowlands (E. Rutherford, New Jersey) and the Kentucky Jockey Club in the slop at Churchill Downs

(Louisville, Kentucky). He also came in second to CAPTAIN BODGIT in the Laurel Futurity (Laurel, Maryland). In 1997, he won the Whirlaway at Aqueduct (Ozone Park, New York) and the Battaglia Stakes at Turfway Park (Florence, Kentucky). CONCERTO then scored his biggest victory in the $600,000 Jim Beam Stakes at Turfway Park. George Steinbrenner, owner of the 1996 World Series champion New York Yankees, owns Kinsman Stable. CONCERTO's sire, CHIEF'S CROWN, won the first Breeders Cup race ever run in 1984. Tammaro: "George (the owner) puts a lot of money into this sport and deserves to win a big one. And no, I'm not a baseball manager, so I don't think I'll get fired."

CONFIDE

Sire	PHONE TRICK
Dam	BAG OF TRICKS
Owner	New Farm
Breeder	John Greeley (bred in Kentucky)
Trainer	Ben Perkins

In 1997, CONFIDE raced in four stakes races at Gulfstream Park (Hallandale, Florida) and won two of them: the Spectacular Bid Stakes and the Swale Stakes. Last year, at Laurel, Maryland he lost by a nose to CAPTAIN BODGIT in the six-furlong Bimelech Stakes.

WHERE IS EVERYBODY?

SPECTACULAR BID (Kentucky Derby, Preakness winner 1979) won a stakes race in 1980 as the only competitor. The other entrants scratched out of fear, and SPECTACULAR BID ran around the track by himself. Such a race with only one horse is called a "walkover."

CROMWELL

Sire	A.P. INDY
Dam	RAPPING
Owner	Bob and Beverly Lewis
Breeder	Cliveden Stud (bred in Kentucky)
Trainer	D. Wayne Lukas

CROMWELL, a grandson of leading sire, MR. PROSPECTOR, won his maiden race at Santa Anita (Arcadia, California) in 1997 at a distance of a mile-and-a-sixteenth. In his first stakes race, he finished third in the mile-and-a-sixteenth Rushaway at Turfway Park (Florence, Kentucky). His trainer, D. Wayne Lukas, won the 1996 Kentucky Derby with GRINDSTONE and the 1996 Belmont Stakes with EDITOR'S NOTE. On April 13th, CROMWELL scored a photo finish victory at Keeneland.

CRYPTO STAR

Sire	CRYPTOCLEARANCE
Dam	ONE I LOVE
Owner	D&E Yates
Breeder	H&S Sexton (bred in Kentucky)
Trainer	Wayne Catalano

CRYPTO STAR was second in 1997 in the Risen Star Stakes at the Fair Grounds in New Orleans, Louisiana. Then, with Pat Day riding, he rallied from far behind to win the Louisiana Derby (Fair Grounds) in a three-way photo finish with STOP WATCH and SMOKE GLACKEN. On April 12th, in the $500,000 Arkansas Derby at Oaklawn Park (Hot Springs, Arkansas), CRYPTO STAR again rallied from far off the pace to win in the final yards over PHANTOM ON TOUR and PACIFICBOUNTY. The Arkansas Derby was a roughly run race, with STOP WATCH being squeezed and forced to alter course in the homestretch.

DAN'S PROMISE

Sire	SEATTLE SLEW
Dam	ALYDAR'S PLEASURE
Owner	Brushwood Stable
Breeder	M/M John C. Mabee (bred in Kentucky)
Trainer	William I. Mott

In April of this year, DAN'S PROMISE won a $38,000 distance race by two lengths at Keeneland (Lexington, Kentucky). His grandsire, ALYDAR, came in second to AFFIRMED in all three Triple Crown races in 1978.

DEEDS NOT WORDS

Sire	RUBIANO
Dam	CHARMING TIARA
Owner	Michael Tabor
Breeder	Brilie and White (bred in Kentucky)
Trainer	D. Wayne Lukas

DEEDS NOT WORDS finished third in the Best Pal Stakes in Del Mar, California. In his maiden victory last year he defeated SILVER CHARM by four lengths at Del Mar, California.

DEPUTY COMMANDER

Sire	DEPUTY MINISTER
Dam	ANKA GERMANIA
Owner	Horizon/Jarvis/Mandysland
Breeder	Crystal Springs/Moore/Allred (bred in Kentucky)
Trainer	Wallace Dollase

DEPUTY COMMANDER finished first on March 2nd , but was **disqualified** from a maiden race at Santa Anita (Arcadia, California) in 1997. In his next race on March 16th he won a maiden event by four lengths.

DIXIE FLAG

Sire	DIXIELAND BAND
Dam	THIRTY FLAGS
Owner	Mrs. Richard duPont
Breeder	Bohemia Stable
	(bred in Maryland)
Trainer	H. Allen Jerkens

DIXIE FLAG, a filly, was undefeated in 1996, winning all three races by many lengths. Each time, rider Jean Luc Samyn, needed binoculars to find the second place finisher. Jerkens is a Hall of Fame trainer who pulled off two of the greatest upsets ever. In the first start of 1963, his BEAU PURPLE won the mile-and-a-quarter Widener Handicap (Hialeah, Florida) over five-time Horse of the Year, KELSO. Then, in the 1973 Whitney at Saratoga, New York, Jerkens trained the little-known, ONION, who defeated none other than SECRETARIAT. Ironically, Mrs. duPont owned KELSO. In her first 1997 start, DIXIE FLAG finished third at Gulfstream Park (Hallandale, Florida) to GLITTER WOMAN.

ESTEEMED FRIEND

Sire	GULCH
Dam	CHARLOTTE AMALIE
Owner	Bob & Beverly Lewis
Breeder	North Central Bloodstock & O'Neil
	(bred in Kentucky)
Trainer	D. Wayne Lukas

In 1997, ESTEEMED FRIEND finished third in the Golden Gate Derby (San Francisco, California) and in the Battaglia Stakes at Turfway Park (Florence, Kentucky) behind CONCERTO and STAR OF HALO. His dam was bred in France. Bob and Beverly recently celebrated their fiftieth wedding anniversary.

FREE HOUSE

Sire   SMOKESTER
Dam   FOUNTAIN LAKE
Owner   McCaffery & Toffan
Breeder   McCaffery & Toffan (bred in California)
Trainer   J. Paco Gonzalez

FREE HOUSE was second in the San Vicente Stakes at Santa Anita (Arcadia, California) in 1997. Then, this grey won the Grade II San Felipe (Santa Anita) with David Flores riding. In the San Felipe, FREE HOUSE took the lead at the beginning of the home stretch and held off second-place finisher, SILVER CHARM. Then on April 5th, FREE HOUSE scored his biggest victory, a photo finish win in the Santa Anita Derby with SILVER CHARM once again finishing second. Gonzalez: "This horse had psychological problems for awhile, shying from other horses, but he has matured famously."

FRISK ME NOW

Sire   MISTER FRISKY
Dam   SLEW ME NOW
Owner   Carol Dender
Breeder   Farnsworth Farms
             (bred in Florida)
Trainer   Bobby Durso

Carol Dender, the wife of trainer Bobby Durso, paid only $18,000 for FRISK ME NOW last year. In his first stakes race try ever, in Gulfstream's 1997 Hutcheson Stakes, FRISK ME NOW lit up the tote board, winning at odds of 105 to 1, returning $213.80 for each $2 win bet. He then finished third in the Florida Derby behind CAPTAIN BODGIT and PULPIT. His biggest win came on April 5th in the $200,000 Flamingo at Hialeah Park (Hialeah, Florida). Durso:

"I've been in this business over 30 years and finally have that one big horse. I pray that he stays sound and healthy so my family can have some fun."

FUNONTHERUN

Sire   RUNAWAY GROOM
Dam   ALDEN'S JUANA
Owner   D&H Alpert
Breeder   D. E. Cook (bred in Kentucky)
Trainer   Melvin F. Stute

This grey colt won the San Rafael Stakes in 1997 at Santa Anita (Arcadia, California), running the one mile in 1 minute and 36 seconds. He also finished third this year in Santa Anita's San Vicente. Although greys, such as SPECTACULAR BID have won Triple Crown races, the most famous grey, NATIVE DANCER, suffered his only lifetime defeat in the Kentucky Derby to a horse named DARK STAR. FUNONTHERUN's owners include Herb Alpert, Grammy-winning musician of Tijuana Brass fame. Stute: "After most of his races, he limps back to the winner's circle, but this must just be his weird habit. He races perfectly sound."

GLITTER WOMAN

Sire   GLITTERMAN
Dam   CAROL'S FOLLY
Owner   Joseph Allen
Breeder   Golden Orb and
    Schwartz
    (bred in Florida)
Trainer   Claude McGaughey

GLITTER WOMAN won three stakes races at Gulfstream Park

(Hallandale, Florida) in early 1997. Her winning margins, combined, were a whopping 26 lengths. She defeated, among others, STORM SONG and DIXIE FLAG. Then she shipped to Keeneland (Lexington, Kentucky) for another easy win in the $500,000 Grade I Ashland Stakes at a mile-and-a-sixteenth. Her sire, GLITTERMAN, is known as a sire of **sprinters**. This daughter, however, doesn't realize she's not supposed to like long races. Let's hope she doesn't learn to read.

GOLD TRIBUTE

Sire	MR. PROSPECTOR
Dam	DANCING TRIBUTE
Owner	Lewis/Magnier/Tabor
Breeder	Mr. and Mrs. J. C. Mabee (bred in Kentucky)
Trainer	D. Wayne Lukas

In 1996, GOLD TRIBUTE finished second in the Del Mar Futurity (Del Mar, California) to SILVER CHARM and third in the Champagne Stakes at Belmont Park (Elmont, New York). He then finished sixth in the Breeders Cup Juvenile at Woodbine (Canada).

HAMILTON CREEK

Sire	FORTUNATE PROSPECT
Dam	RULERS MOM
Owner	Jess Yawitz
Breeder	Sucher Stables (bred in Florida)
Trainer	Phil Hauswald

HAMILTON CREEK won an allowance race at Gulfstream Park (Hallandale, Florida) in 1997 and then came in second to TRAITOR in the OBS Champion Stakes at Ocala Florida Training Center, losing a photo finish.

HE KEPT LOOKING BACK FOR BILLY

Sometimes, when trying to predict who will win the Triple Crown, a horse's racing history doesn't count for much. SIR BARTON, who won the first Triple Crown in 1919, had never won a race before the Kentucky Derby. SIR BARTON wasn't supposed to win; he was supposed to set the pace in the Derby for his stablemate, BILLY KELLY. SIR BARTON went on to win a number of races, but in the same year that he won the Triple Crown, SIR BARTON was beaten by none other than the great MAN O' WAR. The two beautiful chestnuts competed at Kenilworth Park in Windsor, Ontario.

HELLO

Sire	LYCIUS
Dam	ITQAN
Owner	Al and Sandy Kirkwood
Breeder	H. Volz (bred in Ireland)
Trainer	Ron McAnally

This bay colt, born in Ireland, raced on grass surfaces last year in England and Italy. In his American stakes debut this year in the Santa Catalina Stakes at Santa Anita (Arcadia, California). HELLO carried jockey Chris McCarron to victory over top-class rivals, such as BOSTON HARBOR, who was voted last year's two-year-old champion. In the Santa Anita Derby on April 5th, HELLO finished third behind FREE HOUSE and SILVER CHARM. McAnally: "He's a small horse who needs extra time between his races."

HOLZMEISTER

Sire	WOODMAN
Dam	HARBOUR CLUB
Owner	Frank Stronach
Breeder	M.F. Seltzer (bred in Kentucky)
Trainer	Richard Mandella

HOLZMEISTER won the 1996 Hawthorne Juvenile in Chicago by 17 lengths in the mud. He suffered a brutal trip in the San Felipe at Santa Anita (Arcadia, California) getting bumped, forced wide, and inadvertently hit on the head by the whip of a rival jockey.

IN CC'S HONOR

Sire	ALLEN'S PROSPECT
Dam	QUALITY GAL
Owner	Childs and Childs Stable
Breeder	R. B. Davis (bred in Maryland)
Trainer	Donald H. Barr

After IN CC'S HONOR won his first lifetime race in 1996 by 15 lengths, the owners received a $400,000 offer for this gelding. They turned it down (good thinking!). In 1997, he won a mile-and-one-eighth non-stakes race and then the Herat Stakes at a mile-and-a-sixteenth (both at Laurel Park, Maryland), In the

Herat, IN CC'S HONOR led the entire way in deep slop. He then won the Stryker Stakes in front-running fashion at Laurel. At Turfway Park (Florence Kentucky), he was a clear second to ANET in the Rushaway.

JACK FLASH

Sire	SOVEREIGN DANCER
Dam	WHOW
Owner	Dogwood Stable
Breeder	W. Farish & Hermitage Farm (bred in Kentucky)
Trainer	Nicholas P. Zito

JACK FLASH is a grandson of SPECTACULAR BID, who won the Kentucky Derby and Preakness in 1979. SPECTACULAR BID was the last betting favorite to be victorious in the Kentucky Derby. JACK FLASH finished fourth in the Florida Derby at Gulfstream Park (Hallandale, Florida). Then, despite running against a bias that favored front runners at Turfway Park (Florence, Kentucky), JACK FLASH finished a fast-closing second in the Jim Beam to CONCERTO.

JULES

Sire	FORTY NINER
Dam	BONITA FRANCITA
Owner	Jayeff B. Stables
Breeder	Jayeff B. Stables
	(bred in Kentucky)
Trainer	Alan Goldberg

In 1996, while racing at Aqueduct (Ozone Park, New York), JULES won the Nashua over SHAMMY DAVIS and finished second in both the Remsen (losing to THE SILVER MOVE) and in the Cowdin. In 1997, JULES set the early pace and finished fourth in the Jim Beam at Turfway Park (Florence, Kentucky).

KEEP IT STRAIT
Sire	COUNTRY PINE
Dam	CHOU CHOU
Owner	Marvin and Gil Delfiner
Breeder	Donna Wormser (bred in Florida)
Trainer	Joseph Pierce

KEEP IT STRAIT finished third in the Tropical Park Derby to ARTHUR L. at Calder Race Course (Miami, Florida). In the Everglades Stakes at Hialeah, Florida, with jockey Jose Ferrer up, he rallied from three zip codes away to finish third.

KING CRIMSON
Sire	CAPOTE
Dam	WINTERS' LOVE
Owner	Griffiths, Henderson & Weston
Breeder	North Central Blood Stock (bred in Kentucky)
Trainer	Riley Griffiths

KING CRIMSON won an allowance race at Santa Anita (Arcadia, California) and then came in third in that track's San Felipe Stakes losing to FREE HOUSE and SILVER CHARM.

KING OF SWING
        Sire   DIXIELAND BAND
        Dam   STAR GEM
        Owner   Columbine and Stronach
        Breeder   Double J Farm (bred in Kentucky)
        Trainer   Richard Mandella
KING OF SWING won his first two lifetime races in 1996. In his
1997 debut, he finished a troubled third in the Pirate Cove Stakes
on the grass at Santa Anita (Arcadia, California). He then had
another troubled trip when finishing second in a grass race.

LEESTOWN
        Sire   SEATTLE SLEW
        Dam   BRIGHT CANDLES
        Owner   Overbrook Farm
        Breeder   P. M. Rosebrock (bred in Maryland)
        Trainer   D. Wayne Lukas
LEESTOWN finished third in the 1996 Tremont Stakes at Belmont
Park (Elmont, New York). His sire, SEATTLE SLEW, won the 1977
Triple Crown.

FIDDLE, TROMBONE, DRUMS

*DIXIELAND BAND, a Stakes winner and quite a character, is
also the sire of 1997 contenders DIXIE FLAG and KING OF
SWING. DIXIELAND BAND loved to run, but he had a bad
back. So, when he finished a race (usually in first place), he
went back to his stall and laid down, while handlers used
acupuncture and other means to ease the pain in his back. After
a few days of treatment, DIXIELAND BAND was ready to begin
training for his next race. His progeny have a tendency not to
want other horses in front of them, a trait that's a definite plus.*

MICHELLE'SALLHANDS

Sire	SLEWACIDE
Dam	HARRY'S HAZE
Owner	K. and M. Zacco
Breeder	Mario Zacco (bred in Florida)
Trainer	Mario Zacco

In 1996, while still a maiden, MICHELLE'SALLHANDS finished second in a Florida Stallion Stakes race at Calder Race Course (Miami, Florida), placing in front of BLAZING SWORD. In 1997, he won his first race (at seven furlongs) at Gulfstream Park (Hallandale, Florida). He also finished third in the Flamingo at Hialeah Park (Hialeah, Florida) on April 5th, a race won by FRISK ME NOW.

ORDWAY

Sire	SALT LAKE
Dam	PRICELESS COUNTESS
Owner	Dileo, Punk, and Claiborne
Breeder	Lantern Hill (bred in Kentucky)
Trainer	Dave Donk

ORDWAY was a stakes winner in New York in 1996. He fared poorly in the Hutcheson Stakes at Gulfstream Park (Hallandale, Florida) when he reportedly swallowed his tongue. Donk: "He didn't like the warm weather in Florida, so we decided to finish his Triple Crown preparation in New York." Subsequently, in Aqueduct's Gotham Stakes (Ozone Park, New York), Ordway was a fast-closing second to SMOKIN MEL. Donk was formerly an assistant trainer under Woody Stephens.

PACIFICBOUNTY

Sire	PIRATE'S BOUNTY
Dam	FAST KATIE
Owner	Grey & Harris
Breeder	Ocean Air (bred in California)
Trainer	Walter Greenman

In 1997, PACIFICBOUNTY won the Golden Gate Derby at Golden Gate in San Francisco, California and the El Camino Real Derby at Bay Meadows, also in San Francisco.

PARTNER'S HERO

Sire	DANZIG
Dam	SAFELY HOME
Owner	Horton Stables, Inc.
Breeder	Gilman, Hayden and David (bred in Maryland)
Trainer	D. Wayne Lukas

PARTNER'S HERO finished second in 1996 in the Iroquois Stakes in Kentucky. This year he was an easy winner in a seven-furlong allowance race at Keeneland (Lexington, Kentucky).

PENNANT FLAG

Sire	SUMMER SQUALL
Dam	FOLD THAT FLAG
Owner	W.S. Farish
Breeder	W. S. Farish (bred in Kentucky)
Trainer	Neil Howard

PENNANT FLAG won his debut race at Gulfstream Park (Hallandale, Florida). His sire, SUMMER SQUALL, won the 1990 Preakness.

PHANTOM ON TOUR

Sire	TOUR D'OR
Dam	WHITE WOOL SOCKS
Owner	W. Cal Partee
Breeder	Lou Ann Baker (bred in Ohio)
Trainer	Lynn Whiting

PHANTOM ON TOUR has won stakes races at three different race tracks: Beulah Park (Ohio), Calder Race Course (Florida), and Oaklawn Park (Arkansas). His most impressive victory was in the Rebel at Oaklawn Park when he drew away in the stretch to win by a widening margin. In his brief career, he has been ridden by five different jockeys: Wilfredo Lozano, Victor Molina, Jason Lumpkins, Eibar Coa, and Larry Melancon. Partee and Whiting won the 1992 Kentucky Derby with LIL E. TEE.

PITKIN COUNTY

Sire	PINE BLUFF
Dam	RUB AL KHALI
Owner	John C. Oxley
Breeder	Gainesway Thoroughbred Ltd. (bred in Kentucky)
Trainer	John Ward, Jr.

PITKIN COUNTY won his first career race impressively at Hialeah Park (Hialeah, Florida). Despite a poor start, this chestnut grandson of MR. PROSPECTOR raced eight-wide throughout to win as the overwhelming 3 to 5 favorite. Ward: "PITKIN COUNTY is bred to race long distances and would probably enjoy racing the one-and-one-half mile Belmont Stakes." Oxley owned two horses that ran in the 1995 Kentucky Derby, JAMBALAYA JAZZ and PYRAMID PEAK.

P.T. INDY

Sire	A.P. INDY
Dam	RELUCTANT GUEST
Owner	R. S. Folsom
Breeder	R. S. Folsom (bred in Kentucky)
Trainer	Richard Mandella

P.T. INDY won the Pirate Cove Stakes on grass at Santa Anita (Arcadia, California) in 1997, defeating KING OF SWING and ANET. He was then unplaced in the Santa Anita Derby (Arcadia, California).

PULPIT

Sire	A.P. INDY
Dam	PREACH
Owner	Claiborne Farm
Breeder	Claiborne Farm (bred in Kentucky)
Trainer	Frank L. Brothers

This bay colt, a grandson of Triple Crown winner, SEATTLE SLEW, did not race as a two-year-old. The last Kentucky Derby winner who did not race as a two-year-old was APOLLO who scored back in 1882. PULPIT won his first two races at Gulfstream Park (Hallandale, Florida) by over 14 lengths. He then won the Grade II Fountain of Youth Stakes at Gulfstream Park as the favorite with Shane Sellers riding, defeating BLAZING SWORD and CAPTAIN BODGIT. In his first two races, PULPIT led from gate to wire. In the Fountain of Youth, he proved his versatility by rallying from off the pace to win this mile-and-a-sixteenth prep for the Florida Derby at Gulfstream Park. In the Florida Derby, however, despite being the overwhelming public choice, PULPIT finished second to CAPTAIN BODGIT. On April 12th, PULPIT (first time with Lasix) won the Blue Grass at Keeneland over ACCEPTABLE.

RED JADE

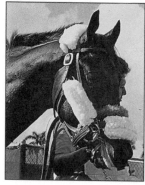

Sire	JADE HUNTER
Dam	LUBBOCK
Owner	Dogwood Stable
Breeder	Allen Paulson
	(bred in Florida)
Trainer	Nicholas P. Zito

RED JADE scored for the first time in 1997 at Gulfstream Park (Hallandale, Florida), then subsequently finished second to PULPIT in a non-stakes race.

RICHTER SCALE

Sire	HABITONY
Dam	DEVINE PET
Owner	N&R Kaster
Breeder	Clydene Boots (bred in California)
Trainer	Patrick Byrne

RICHTER SCALE won his maiden race at Ellis Park in 1996. In his 1997 debut, he won the six-furlong Surfside Stakes at Hialeah Park (Hialeah, Florida).

RUNNING STAG

Sire	COZZENE
Dam	FRUHLINSTAG
Owner	Derek Crowson
Breeder	Juddmonte (bred in Kentucky)
Trainer	Phil Mitchell

RUNNING STAG competed unsuccessfully in France in 1996 while racing on grass surfaces. In 1997, he switched to the dirt at Lingfield (England), where he won the Atlanta Maiden by seven lengths.

SHAMMY DAVIS

Sire	TEMPERENCE HILL
Dam	SISSY SHAM
Owner	Fox Hill Farm
Breeder	Hidden Lane Farm
	(bred in Pennsylvania)
Trainer	Nicholas P. Zito

SHAMMY DAVIS was second in the Nashua Stakes at Aqueduct (Ozone Park, New York) in 1996. In 1997, he finished a close third to CONCERTO in the Jim Beam at Turfway Park (Florence, Kentucky), despite hurdling over a fallen horse. His trainer, Nicholas P. Zito, won the Kentucky Derby in 1991 and 1994.

SHARP CAT

Sire	STORM CAT
Dam	IN NEON
Owner	Ahmed Salman
Breeder	John Franks (bred in Kentucky)
Trainer	D. Wayne Lukas

In 1996, SHARP CAT won the Matron at Belmont Park (Elmont, New York), then was unplaced in the Breeders Cup Juvenile Fillies before finishing the year with a victory in Hollywood Park's Hollywood Starlet Stakes in California. Her total earnings in 1996 exceeded $500,000. In 1997, she won the Santa Ysabel, Las Virgenes and Santa Anita Oaks at Santa Anita (Arcadia, California)—all with Corey Nakatani as her jockey. In her first try against males, she led early but tired to finish unplaced in the Santa Anita Derby. Her trainer, D. Wayne Lukas, has a history of saddling fillies in the Kentucky Derby, most recently with SERENA'S SONG in 1996. The Lukas-trained filly, WINNING COLORS, won the Derby in 1988. SHARP CAT's owner, Ahmed Salman, who races under the *nom de course* The Thoroughbred Corporation, is a member of the Saudi royal family. He also owns horses in Europe and the Middle East. Salman has a 300-acre horse farm in Riyadh, Saudi Arabia.

SILVER CHARM

Sire	SILVER BUCK
Dam	BONNIE'S POKER
Owner	Bob and Beverly Lewis
Breeder	Mary Wootton (bred in Florida)
Trainer	Bob Baffert

In 1996, SILVER CHARM won the Del Mar Futurity at Del Mar, California. In 1997, he stayed on the inside rail all the way when winning the San Vicente Stakes at Santa Anita (Arcadia, California). In his next race, the San Felipe (Santa Anita), he was a fast-rallying second to FREE HOUSE. Then in the Santa Anita Derby (Arcadia, California) SILVER CHARM lost again to FREE HOUSE in a photo finish. Bob and Beverly Lewis owned SERENA'S SONG, the lone filly to compete in the 1996 Kentucky Derby. Trainer Bob Baffert trained CAVONNIER, who finished second in the 1996 Kentucky Derby to GRINDSTONE.

APTLY NAMED

MAN O' WAR didn't win the Triple Crown, but he did become a legend, winning 20 of 21 races. He lost only once (to a horse named UPSET) when he was bumped and jostled while racing in the pack in the Sanford Stakes at Saratoga. Almost twenty years later, one of MAN O' WAR's sons, WAR ADMIRAL, did sweep the Triple Crown in fine fashion. Papa would have been proud.

SMOKE GLACKEN

Sire	TWO PUNCH
Dam	MAJESTY'S CROWN
Owner	Karkenny/Levy/Roberts
Breeder	P.M. Rosebrock (bred in Maryland)
Trainer	Henry Carroll

In 1996, this grey won Monmouth Park's (Oceanport, New Jersey) Tyro and Sapling Stakes, and then he won the Grade I Hopeful Stakes at Saratoga (Saratoga Springs, New York). In 1997, he scored with victories in the Fair Grounds' (New Orleans, Louisiana), Black Gold Stakes, and the Oaklawn Park (Hot Springs, Arkansas) Southwest Stakes and Mountain Valley Stakes. Part-owner Robert Levy owned champion sprinter HOUSEBUSTER. In the Southwest, SMOKE GLACKEN's first race around two turns, he won by eight lengths. He then finished third in a three-way photo finish in the Louisiana Derby (Fair Grounds), losing to CRYPTO STAR and STOP WATCH.

SMOKIN MEL

Sire	PHONE ORDER
Dam	SHE'S SMOKIN
Owner	S. Port and E. Wachtel
Breeder	Annabelle Stute (bred in Washington)
Trainer	John DiStefano

SMOKIN MEL, a grey, won two claiming races last year in California and could have been purchased by anyone for $32,000. He then came in second in the San Miguel Stakes at Santa Anita (Arcadia, California). This year, SMOKIN MEL won the $200,000 Gotham Stakes at Aqueduct (Ozone Park, New York) at odds of 15 to 1 under jockey John Velazquez, who had been the regular rider of second-place-finisher, ORDWAY.

CHICKEN FLAMINGO

The 1966 Flamingo Stakes is known as "The Chicken Flamingo" because Hialeah racetrack president Eugene Mori decided to make it a non-betting race so that the track would not lose money when huge favorite, and champion racehorse, BUCKPASSER, was entered to run. BUCKPASSER subsequently escaped with a slim nose win over second place finisher, ABE'S HOPE.

SOCIAL PILLAR

Sire	GONE WEST
Dam	SOCIAL COLUMN
Owner	Mark Stanley
Breeder	Juddmonte (bred in Kentucky)
Trainer	W. Elliott Walden

In 1996, SOCIAL PILLAR won the Billockby Nursery Stakes at Yarmouth (England).

STAR OF HALO

Sire	HALO
Dam	STAR ON THE MOVE
Owner	H&K Biggs
Breeder	Hartland/Oakcliff (bred in Kentucky)
Trainer	Steve Wren

In 1997, STAR OF HALO finished second in the Old Rosebud Stakes at Oaklawn Park (Hot Springs, Arkansas). In the Battaglia Stakes at Turfway Park (Florence, Kentucky), STAR OF HALO lost to CONCERTO.

STOP WATCH

Sire   LORD AT WAR
Dam   WATCH THE TIME
Owner   Claiborne Farm and Adele Dilschneider
Breeder   Fred Seitz (bred in Kentucky)
Trainer   Frank L. Brothers

STOP WATCH garnered his maiden victory by a whopping 12 lengths at Gulfstream Park (Hallandale, Florida) in 1997. He then won an allowance race (non-stakes race) when he rallied from far behind to take the lead just before the finish line. In his first ever stakes race appearance, under jockey Mike Smith, he finished a close second to CRYPTO STAR in the Louisiana Derby at Fair Grounds. His trainer, Brothers, also trains PULPIT.

STORM SONG

Sire   SUMMER SQUALL
Dam   HUM ALONG
Owner   Dogwood Stable
Breeder   Ogden Phipps and
     Will Farish
     (bred in Kentucky)
Trainer   Nicholas P. Zito

With earnings of $898,000 in 1996, STORM SONG's victories included two smaller stakes races and the Breeders Cup Juvenile Fillies when she was ridden by jockey Craig Perret. This bay won the 1996 two-year-old filly championship, the Eclipse Award. On April 5th of this year, STORM SONG finished third in the Ashland Stakes at Keeneland (Lexington, Kentucky). Her trainer, Nicholas P. Zito, won the 1991 Kentucky Derby with STRIKE THE GOLD, the 1994 Kentucky Derby with GO FOR GIN, and last year's Preakness with LOUIS QUATORZE.

SWAGGER

Sire	MAJOR MORAN
Dam	I'M A KITTY KAT
Owner	Sibling Stable
Breeder	B. and S. Tortora (bred in Florida)
Trainer	Graham Maxwell

Despite being bred for longer distances, SWAGGER raced formidably in a sprint debut at Gulfstream Park (Hallandale, Florida). Then, he won impressively in a March maiden race at Hialeah Park (Hialeah, Florida). The victory was SWAGGER's first attempt at over a mile in distance.

THE SILVER MOVE

Sire	SILVER BUCK
Dam	FASHION LIGHT
Owner	E. Silver & Centennial
Breeder	Centaur/Scott (bred in Florida)
Trainer	Linda Rice

THE SILVER MOVE was a stakes winner in 1996 at New York, capturing Aqueduct's Remsen. He finished third in his 1997 debut at Gulfstream Park (Hallandale, Florida) in the seven-furlong Swale Stakes.

TOUCH GOLD

Sire	DEPUTY MINISTER
Dam	PASSING MOOD
Owner	Frank Stronach
Breeder	Holtsinger Inc. (bred in Kentucky)
Trainer	Danny Vella

TOUCH GOLD won a six-furlong race on March 14th at Santa Anita (Arcadia, California).

TRAITOR

Sire   CRYPTOCLEARANCE
Dam   CLEVER BUT COSTLY
Owner   Alfred Vanderbilt
Breeder   Conway and Teinowitz
    (bred in Kentucky)
Trainer   Mary Eppler

In 1996, TRAITOR won the Futurity at Belmont Park (Elmont, New York) and finished second in the Champagne Stakes at Belmont Park. In his first 1997 start, TRAITOR won the $100,000 OBS Champion Stakes at the Ocala Florida Training Center, a non-betting race. This win came despite TRAITOR losing a horseshoe at the beginning of the race. Vanderbilt owned NATIVE DANCER, who suffered his only career defeat in the 1953 Kentucky Derby, which was won by DARK STAR.

VERMILION

Sire   STORM BIRD
Dam   CRYSTAL CREAM
Owner   Farfellow Farms
Breeder   Farfellow Farms (bred in Kentucky)
Trainer   Nicholas P. Zito

This grandson of both NORTHERN DANCER (Kentucky Derby and Preakness winner, 1964) and SECRETARIAT (Triple Crown winner, 1973) was still a maiden in 1996 when he finished third in the Grade II Hollywood Juvenile Championship at Hollywood, California. In his second race this year, he scored his first lifetime victory in the slop at Turfway Park (Florence, Kentucky).

WILD RUSH

Sire WILD AGAIN
Dam ROSE PARK
Owner Frank Stronach
Breeder Ward Pitfield (bred in Kentucky)
Trainer Richard Mandella

WILD RUSH won his first two lifetime starts in 1996 at the Fair Grounds (New Orleans, Louisiana).

WILD TEMPEST

Sire SUMMER SQUALL
Dam MISWILA
Owner William Condren
Breeder Centaur Farms
(bred in Kentucky)
Trainer Nicholas P. Zito

WILD TEMPEST cost $375,000 as a **yearling**. His owner, William Condren, was part owner of two previous Kentucky Derby winners: STRIKE THE GOLD (1991) and GO FOR GIN (1994). WILD TEMPEST had a disappointing career until March 8th, when he won an allowance race at Gulfstream Park (Hallandale, Florida) defeating JULES and SHAMMY DAVIS at odds of 23 to 1 in a four-horse field. This was his first major victory—the first time he raced over one mile and the first time he was ridden by jockey Joe Bravo.

WILD WONDER

Sire	WILD AGAIN
Dam	CAROL'S WONDER
Owner	VHW Stable
Breeder	Verne Winchell (bred in Kentucky)
Trainer	Greg Gilchrist

In 1997, WILD WONDER won the Redwood and Foster City Stakes races at Bay Meadows (San Francisco, California). He finished second to PACIFICBOUNTY in the El Camino Real Derby in San Francisco and third to SMOKIN MEL in Aqueduct's Gotham Stakes (Ozone Park, New York).

WRIGHTWOOD

Sire	SEATTLE SLEW
Dam	WINTER SPARKLE
Owner	Bob & Beverly Lewis
Breeder	Quiet Entry Farm (bred in Kentucky)
Trainer	D. Wayne Lukas

In 1996, WRIGHTWOOD was third in the Haggin Stakes at Hollywood Park, California. In January of this year, he won a $46,000 allowance race at Santa Anita (Arcadia, California). Lukas: "This horse is an impressive-looking individual. He might surprise every-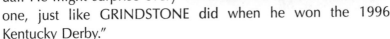one, just like GRINDSTONE did when he won the 1996 Kentucky Derby."

ZEDE

Sire   STRAWBERRY ROAD
Dam   INDEX'S
Owner   Allen Paulson
Breeder   Allen Paulson
(bred in Kentucky)
Trainer   William I. Mott

Trainer Mott and owner Paulson combined to bring us CIGAR, who was horse racing's Horse of the Year in both 1995 and 1996. With jockey Jerry Bailey, ZEDE won the Tampa Bay Derby at Tampa Bay Downs (Tampa, Florida).

WON A BUCK

The Ohio Derby, Jersey Derby, and Pennsylvania Derby are held after the running of the Kentucky Derby. In 1985, SPEND A BUCK won the Kentucky Derby but opted to pass the Preakness (and all Triple Crown hopes) in order to run the Jersey Derby at Garden State Park (Cherry Hill, New Jersey), where he won a purse in excess of $2 million.

IN FOCUS

WHIRLAWAY won only two of his four races in Florida the winter before the 1941 Kentucky Derby. He had a tendency to go far wide in the turn prior to the **homestretch**. With the aid of **blinkers** and the great jockey, Eddie Arcaro, WHIRLAWAY won the Derby by eight lengths in record time and went on to win the Triple Crown.

NOTES

NOTES

HORSE TALK GLOSSARY

Allowance Race   A type of race where the horses are allowed to carry weights based on their recent performances, e.g., a horse who has won twice in the past month would carry 122 pounds, while his competitors would carry 117 pounds. Allowance race purses are less than those in **stakes** races.

Bay   A brown horse.

Betting/Wagering   As a spectator, you don't have to bet on the races. The simplest bets are to pick a horse to win the race (a "win" bet); come in first or second (a "place" bet); or come in first, second or third (a "show" bet). The rewards are commensurate with the risk you are willing to take. The "win" bet pays the most, with "place" paying less, and "show" paying the least of the three wagers. For more complicated bets, see **Double, Exacta** and **Trifecta.**

Blinkers   A head hood that keeps a horse's vision and attention straight ahead.

Breeder   The person who pre-selects the **sire** and **dam** of a horse, and who, in most cases, owns the horse when it is born.

Broken

A young horse is broken when he is initially trained to accept a saddle and a rider.

Chestnut

A light, reddish-brown horse.

Claiming

A race where the owner risks losing his horse to a buyer who "claims" him just prior to the race. The old owner receives any purse earnings, the new owner walks away with the animal at the price stated in the conditions of the race. For example, in a $25,000 claiming race, all horses in the event can be claimed for that amount. One of the greatest horses of all time was STYMIE, who was claimed for $1,500 early in his career and won over $900,000.

Colt

A male horse four years of age or less. After he becomes five, he is just referred to as a horse.

Connections

Technically, the owners of a horse, but also may refer to people in a supporting role, such as trainers, grooms, exercise riders, and friends of the owners.

Dam

The mother of a horse.

Derby

A **stakes** race for three-year-olds, open to both male and female horses.

Disqualify

A horse is disqualified if it bumps or impedes another horse during the course of the race. The disqualified horse is placed behind the impeded horse in the order of finish.

Double

A bet that requires you to select the winners of two consecutive races.

Exacta

A bet that requires you to pick the first two horses to finish a single race.

Filly

A female horse four years of age or less. A female five years or older is referred to as a mare.

Furlong

An eighth of a mile, 220 yards. A six furlong race is contested at a distance of three-quarters of a mile; an eight furlong race is at one mile. The Kentucky Derby, at one-and-a-quarter miles, is a ten furlong race. Originally, a furlong was the length of a furrow in a common field.

Gelding

A castrated male horse (Ouch!). This is done to make headstrong horses more tractable for the training regimen. (Double ouch!).

Homestretch

As horses approach the finish line, they are said to be running in the homestretch, or stretch.

Maiden

Definitely not a blushing bride. A maiden is a horse of either sex (even a **gelding!**) who has never won a race.

Oaks	A stakes race for three-year-old **fillies.**
Paddock	The area for fan viewing adjacent to the grandstand where horses are saddled and jockeys mount them immediately prior to a race.
Post Position	The assigned stall in a starting gate; e.g., the number one post position is closest to the inside rail, and the number twelve post position in a 12 horse race would be furthest from the inside rail. Post positions are drawn by lot approximately 48 hours before a race.
Post-time	The time at which a race is scheduled to begin, e.g., 5:44 P.M. Usually, a racetrack will have about ten races per day, spaced approximately 25 to 30 minutes apart.
Purse	The money put up by a racetrack and distributed to the horses that compete in a race. Usually, 60 percent of a purse is given to the winner, 20 percent to the second finisher (place), and 10 percent to the third finisher (show). The remaining money may be distributed to the fourth and fifth place finishers or to all the remaining competitors in a race.
Roan	A horse with mostly white hairs and some red.

Scratched	When a horse is entered in a race and then, for whatever reason, does not run in the race, it is said to have been scratched or declared from the running.
Shadow Roll	A noseband placed under the horse's eyes to prevent him from suddenly seeing shadows during a race (some horses will jump over shadows).
Sire	The father of a horse.
Soundness	A horse is sound when he has no lameness or soreness in his legs.
Sprinter	A horse that performs best at short distances (for example, five or six furlongs).
Stakes Race	A race with a high dollar value to its purse; only the best horses compete in stakes races.
Trifecta	A bet that requires you to select the first three horses to finish in a single race.
Turf Racing	Racing over a grass surface, versus the track surfaces of dirt, sand, and loam on which most U.S. races are run.
Vetted Out	When a veterinarian certifies that a horse has no illness or infirmity that would prevent him from racing competitively.
Yearling	A one-year-old horse.

ABOUT THE AUTHOR/PHOTOGRAPHER

Anita Scialli is a horse-lover, award-winning photographer and sports enthusiast. For many years, she used her master's degree in education to teach people with developmental disabilities. Since the early eighties, she has resided in south Florida and currently owns a real estate brokerage in Islamorada, the Florida Keys.

This book was created from Ms. Scialli's frustration with the lack of information available to racing fans. As Ms. Scialli expresses it, "Average fans go to the races and don't have a clue as to who's who or what's what—as they would at football, baseball or hockey games. A fan can't pick up a newspaper or turn on a television set and learn anything about the sport. There is little media coverage. I wanted to make it easier for others to enjoy thoroughbred racing as I do. I would love to have had this book in my hands in the years before I became a thoroughbred owner. The more you understand this sport, the more it becomes a passion." Ms. Scialli would enjoy hearing from readers about *Inside Track.* She can be reached at 305-664-1141. If her dog, Nikki, answers, please leave a voice mail.

ABOVE: The author with 1997 contender CAPTAIN BODGIT. ABOVE LEFT: The author with her as yet unnamed two-year-old colt.

ALSO FROM CORMORANT PRESS